W9-BCG-930

DISCARDED

Neptune

by J.P. Bloom

ABDO
PLANETS
Kids

abdopublishing.com

Published by Abdo Kids, a division of ABDO, PO Box 398166, Minneapolis, Minnesota 55439.

Copyright © 2015 by Abdo Consulting Group, Inc. International copyrights reserved in all countries. No part of this book may be reproduced in any form without written permission from the publisher.

Printed in the United States of America, North Mankato, Minnesota.

102014

012015

 THIS BOOK CONTAINS
RECYCLED MATERIALS

Photo Credits: iStock, NASA, Science Source, Shutterstock, Thinkstock

Production Contributors: Teddy Borth, Jennie Forsberg, Grace Hansen

Design Contributors: Laura Rask, Dorothy Toth

Library of Congress Control Number: 2014943781

Cataloging-in-Publication Data

J.P. Bloom.

 Neptune / J.P. Bloom.

   p. cm. -- (Planets)

ISBN 978-1-62970-719-8 (lib. bdg.)

Includes index.

1. Neptune (Planet)--Juvenile literature. 2. Solar system--Juvenile literature.   I. Title.

523.48--dc23

            2014943781

Table of Contents

Neptune

Neptune is a **planet**. Planets **orbit** stars. Planets in our solar system orbit the sun.

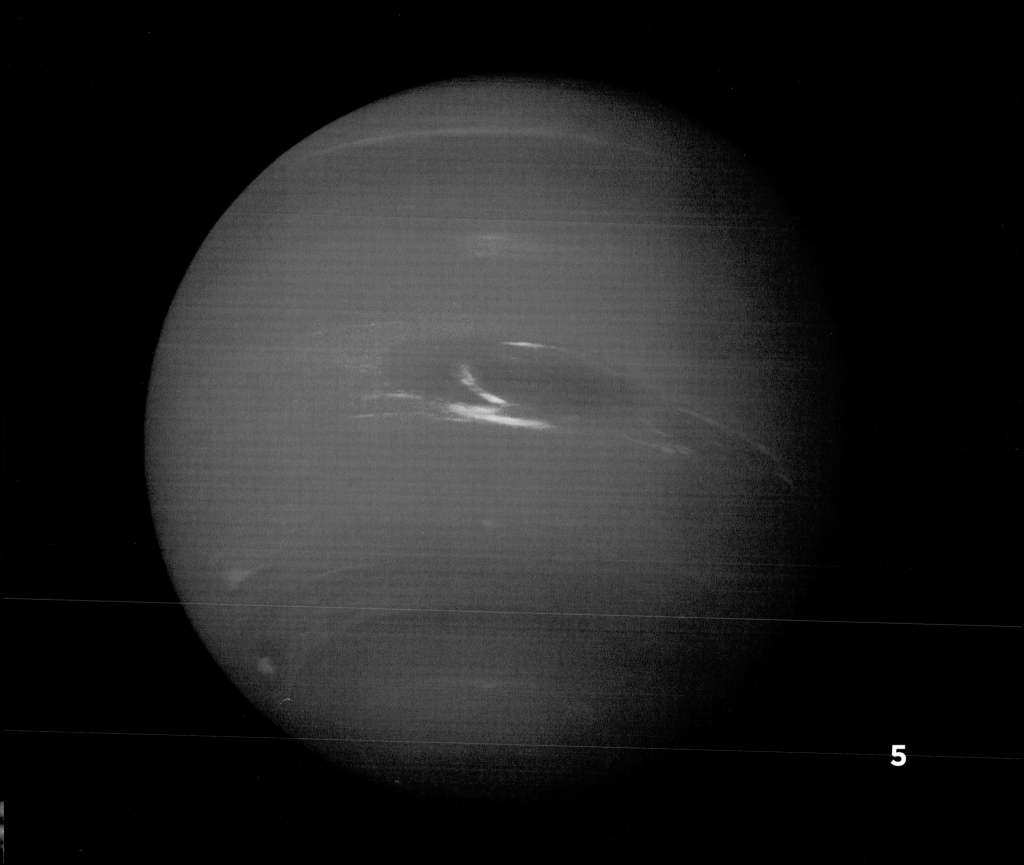

5

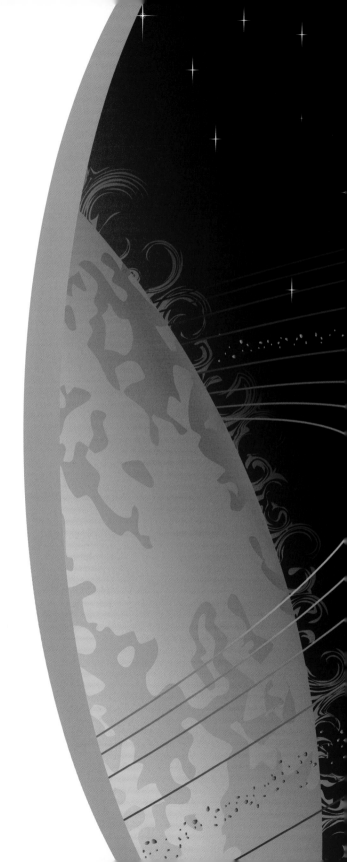

Neptune is the eighth

planet from the sun. It

is about 2.8 billion miles

(4.5 billion km) from the sun.

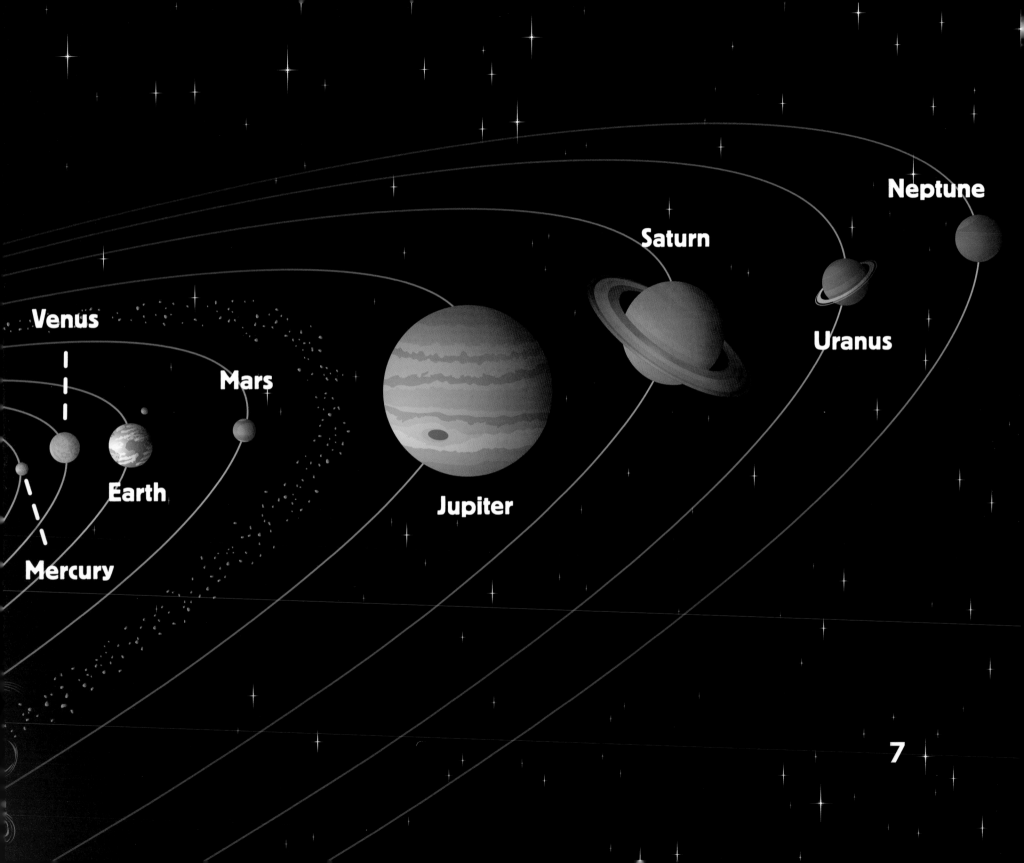

Venus

Mercury

Earth

Mars

Jupiter

Saturn

Uranus

Neptune

Neptune fully orbits the sun every 165 years. One year on Neptune is 165 years on Earth.

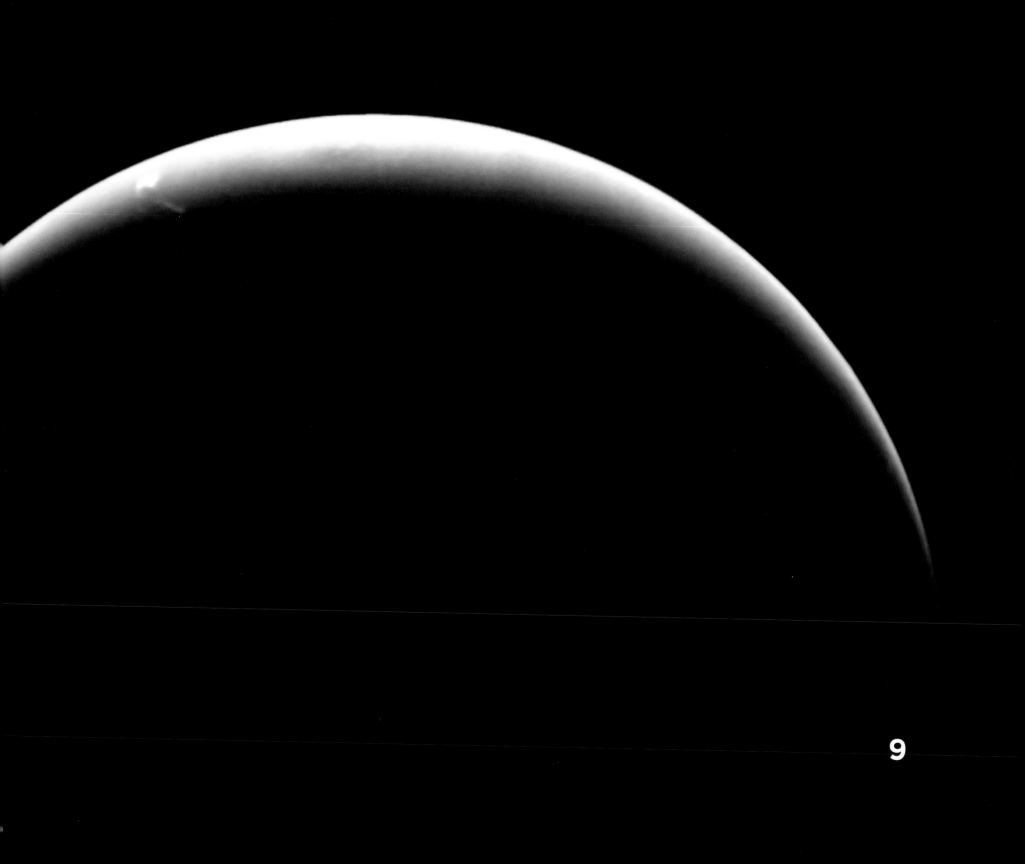

9

Neptune spins while in **orbit**. One full spin takes about 16 hours. One day on Neptune is 16 hours on Earth.

Neptune
30,598 miles   (49,243 km)

Earth
7,918 miles
(12,743 km)

Cold Planet

Neptune is one of the coldest planets. Its average temperature is -353°F (-214°C).

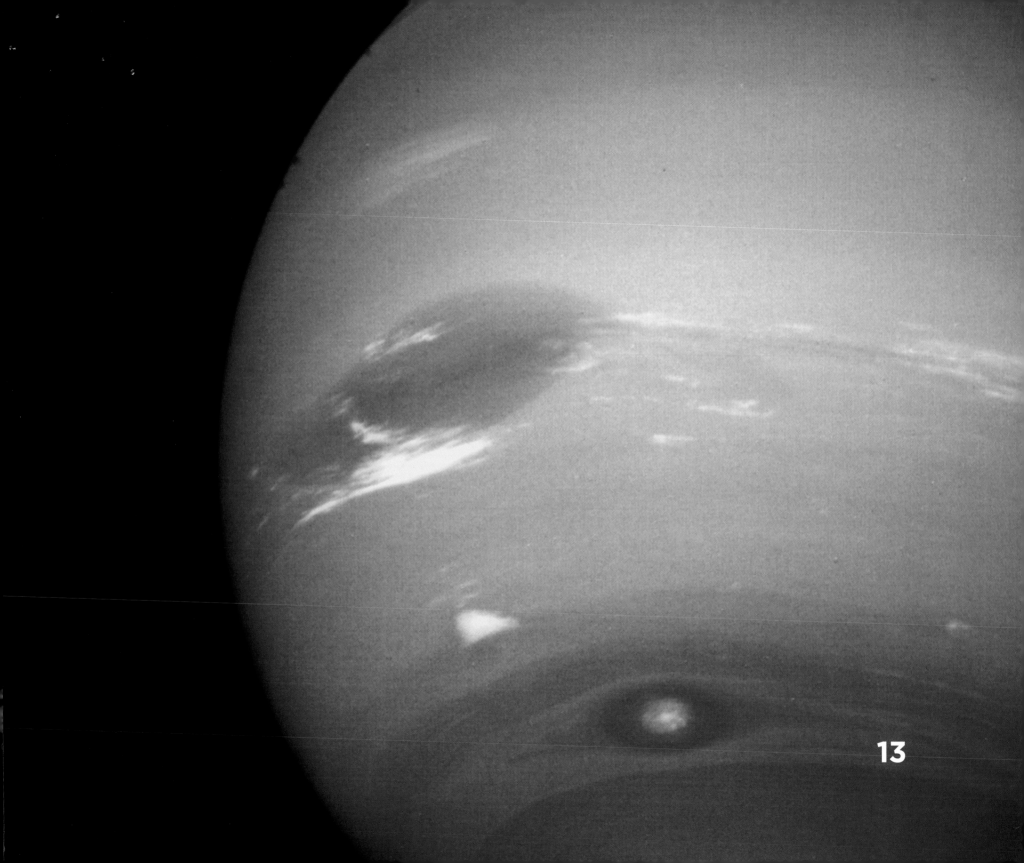

Gas Giant

Neptune is a gas giant. The air is made of gases. The air is mostly hydrogen and helium.

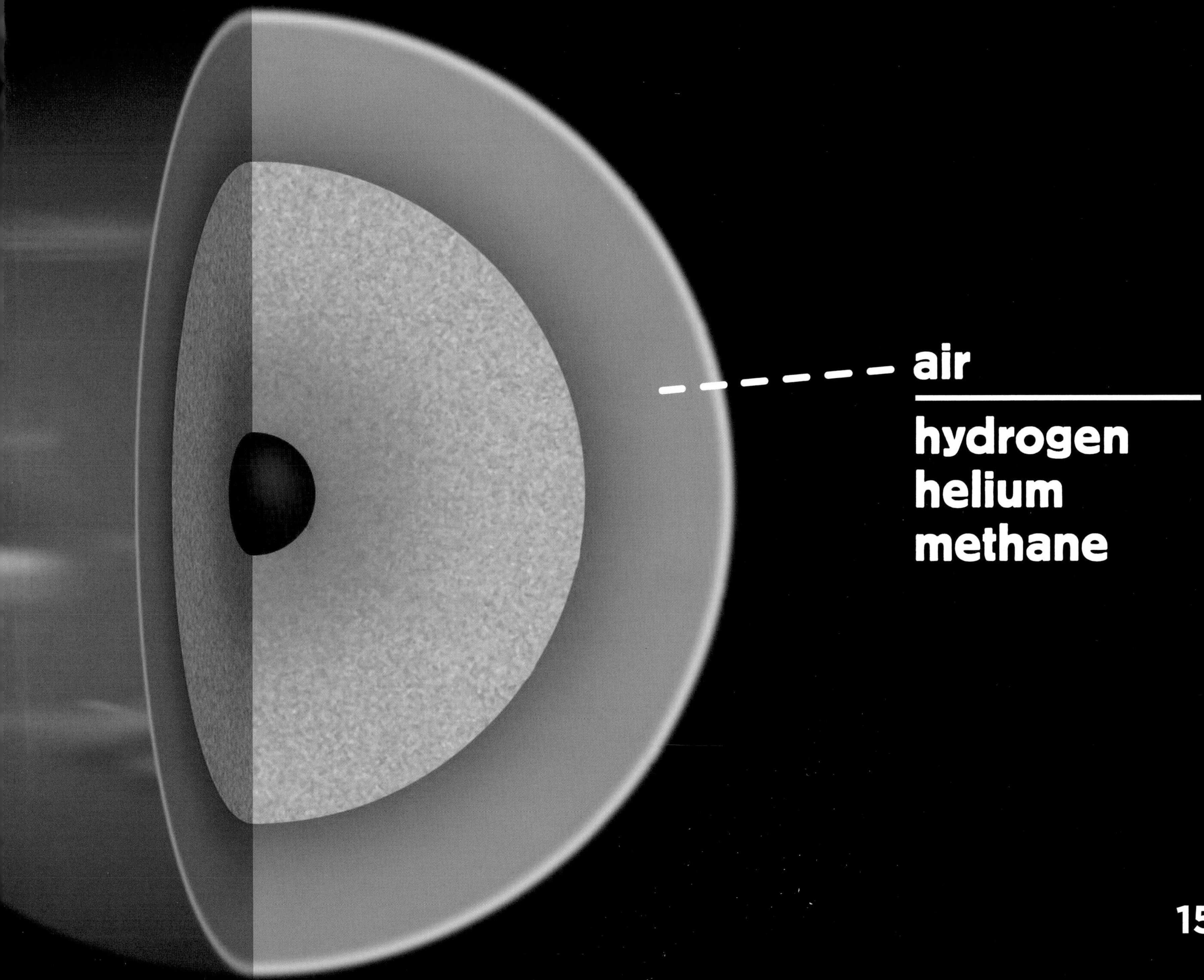

air
_____
hydrogen
helium
methane

Blue Planet

Neptune's air also has methane. Methane **absorbs** red light. This is one reason Neptune is blue.

17

Ice Giant

Neptune is also an ice giant. Its core and mantle are made of rocks and ices.

mantle
_____
water
ammonia
methane ice

core
_____
rock
ice

19

Neptune from Earth

Neptune is very hard to see. You can see Neptune from Earth with a telescope. But you have to know where to look!

More Facts

- Neptune is an ice planet, but it is also a gas planet. Like all gas planets, Neptune has very fast winds and large storms.

- Though they are not easily seen, Neptune has rings that surround it. Neptune's rings are very dark because the sun cannot reflect off of them.

- If you look at Neptune through binoculars, you will not see much. A telescope is the best tool to use to see Neptune in the sky.

Glossary

absorb – to take in or soak up.

binoculars – a tool with a lens for each eye to see objects that are far away.

orbit – the path of a space object as it moves around another space object. To orbit is to follow its path.

planet – a large, round object in space (such as Earth) that travels around a star (such as the sun).

reflect – able to shine light back.

Index

abdokids.com

Use this code to log on to abdokids.com and access crafts, games, videos, and more!

Abdo Kids Code:
PNK7198